# The Meal Prep Queen's Cookbook

## A Meal Prep Guide for Healthy Living

KAITLYN MADER

ISBN: 9798311360500 (Paperback)

ISBN: 9798312998085 (Hardcover)



**Cover Photo Credit: AJ Norton**

I started my job as a personal trainer in July of 2020 after a fifteen-year career in the food industry. At this time, I was more than years into my "I'm-tired-of-my-own-crap" journey but more than a decade into my struggles with losing weight and keeping it off.

When I decided I was tired of the back and forth, I found a program I could follow at home that started teaching me about better portion control and meal prepping. As I was still working in the food industry, it became apparent that meal prepping would be beneficial to keeping me on track with nutrition—at least better on track.

It was a struggle trying to figure out how to put meals together to fit my goals and keep me fueled throughout the days, especially with my rocky relationship with food, emotions, and an inconsistent schedule. Prepping meals ahead of time sometimes meant trial and error, which also meant I had plenty of less-than-stellar meals that I ate anyway. I grew up in a "waste not, want not" household, and I wasn't about to waste my own groceries and time if I could help it.

By the time I started working at the gym, meal prepping just became part of my routine and part of who I am. I was creating my own grab-and-go meals, making the healthier option obvious. It wasn't long before my new coworkers had dubbed me the Meal Prep Queen.

There have been days I resented this part of my week. It is sometimes work when I'd rather be doing something else on my day off. When the work week begins, life gets crazy, unexpected schedule changes and meetings come up, and I am always grateful for my healthy grab-and-go meals.

Many of my coworkers, clients, gym members, and followers have requested me to cook for them. There are just not enough hours in the day and days in the week to cook healthy meals for every person's needs and likes. The next best thing is to write the recipes I use regularly to keep me healthy and working toward my fitness goals.

Sharing my knowledge, teaching, and helping others find healthier lifestyles has brought so much meaning to my life, and I hope this book helps you along your journey.

You'll notice in these recipes that there's much to gain, and hopefully, you'll be just as satisfied with the flavors, fullness, and fulfillment you get from them.

# Table of Contents

# Pantry & Fridge Essentials (according to me)

### Pantry

Cooking fat (olive oil, avocado oil, coconut oil, etc.)
Dried herbs and spices
Whole grains (rice, quinoa, amaranth)
Dried or canned beans
Canned tomato products (diced, puree, paste)
Dark chocolate
Cocoa powder
Old-fashioned rolled oats
Maple syrup
Honey (local is best)
Nuts (peanuts, pistachios, almonds, walnuts)
Seeds (chia, flax, pumpkin, etc.)
Onion
Potatoes or sweet potatoes

### Refrigerator/Freezer

Butter, lard
Eggs
Milk of choice
Greek yogurt
Fresh fruit (especially berries)
Vegetables
Minced garlic
Cottage cheese
Block cheddar cheese
Olives
Kosher dill pickles
Ketchup and mustard

# My Favorite Kitchen Tools and Equipment

- **Cast iron pans.** Yes, they need some upkeep, but once you season and maintain them, they're the best, and there are no concerns about the non-stick coating getting into your food.
- **Quality knives.** You'll need a variety of sizes and types for different uses. Find a set that feels good in your hands. I like a heavier handle that's also sturdy.
- **Measuring cups** for dry goods and liquids and the plunger style for stickier items.
- **Food scale.** I'm a former baker, so weighing ingredients comes naturally to me. I also prefer to buy meat in bulk and then portion it according to how I use it.
- **Ninja Food Processor and Blender** for smoothies and quickly mincing vegetables and fruits.
- **Durable cutting boards.** I currently have flexible cutting boards, which work well but also slide around a bit. Place a kitchen towel underneath the board if you run into that same issue.
- **Rimmed baking sheets.** Buy them at a restaurant store if you have one. They're far cheaper there than anywhere else.
- **Glass or stainless steel mixing bowls** of all sizes, and make sure they nest into each other to save space.
- **Small items:** vegetable peeler, measuring spoons, spatulas and spoons, whisk, milk frother, meat thermometer and/or digital thermometer.
- **Meal prep containers.** There are tons of options online, from plastic to glass, compartmentalized to single compartments, and various sizes.
- **Instant Pot or Crock-Pot.** I use an Instant Pot to make yogurt, and my Crock-Pot comes in handy when I have a busy weekend and still have meals to prep.

# BREAKFAST

My personal favorite foods for any time of day

My relationship with food has always been a roller coaster, to say the least. I grew up in the age of the Atkins diet, low fat or no fat. Women had to be super skinny to be healthy and beautiful. I also grew up in an area where everything was covered in browned butter, sauces, and cheese, and portions were limitless. Emotions were either consumed with food or alcohol but rarely dealt with or spoken about. And exercise —well, that was for the jocks and already fit people.

It's no question that I ended up overweight at a young age.

I would often start my days with Pop-Tarts or Toaster Strudel, having snacks instead of an actual meal at school (though let's face it, the school lunches were questionable no matter what you chose). At home, I would often grab the jar of Jif peanut butter (the huge family-sized one with the red pop-top) and a spoon and mindlessly dig in while doing homework.

At dinnertime, I was insatiable, sometimes eating as much as my dad, thinking that was OK or "normal." Let's not forget dessert, too. Ice cream, cookies, donuts, pie... there was almost always something. As a teenager, my mom signed up for L.A. Weightloss, and I went with her a couple of times to her check-ins. I followed her diet plan at home. It didn't last long. First, I remember the diet plan being boring. Secondly, I didn't understand why she and I had to change our eating habits, but no one else in the house did. Somehow, we were supposed to ignore the chips and Oreos in the pantry.

At the same time, I befriended a girl down the street who lived entirely different from me. She was homeschooled, and her mom bought everything organic; they ground their own flour, used unrefined sweeteners, and got milk directly from a farmer down the road. It was my first taste of unprocessed baked goods, and though different, I really liked it! I asked a few questions about what they use and why they are different, and I stuck those bits of information in the back of my mind. I still didn't feel like I could make that change for the whole household. Maybe one day.

# BOOST YOUR SCRAMBLED EGGS

**Serves 1**

## Ingredients

- 2 whole eggs
- 1/3 cup Egg Whites
- 1/4 cup cottage cheese
- Pinch of Pully Wissle P-DuB Rub
- Dash of dried parsley
- 2 dashes of garlic powder

Use a tall blender or immersion blend to combine your ingredients well. Cook over medium heat. They can also be cooked in a Mini Waffle Maker if you're putting them with one of the waffle or pancake recipes.

## Tools/Equipment Needed

- Immersion blender
- Dry or plunger measuring cup
- Liquid measuring cup
- Skillet or mini waffle maker

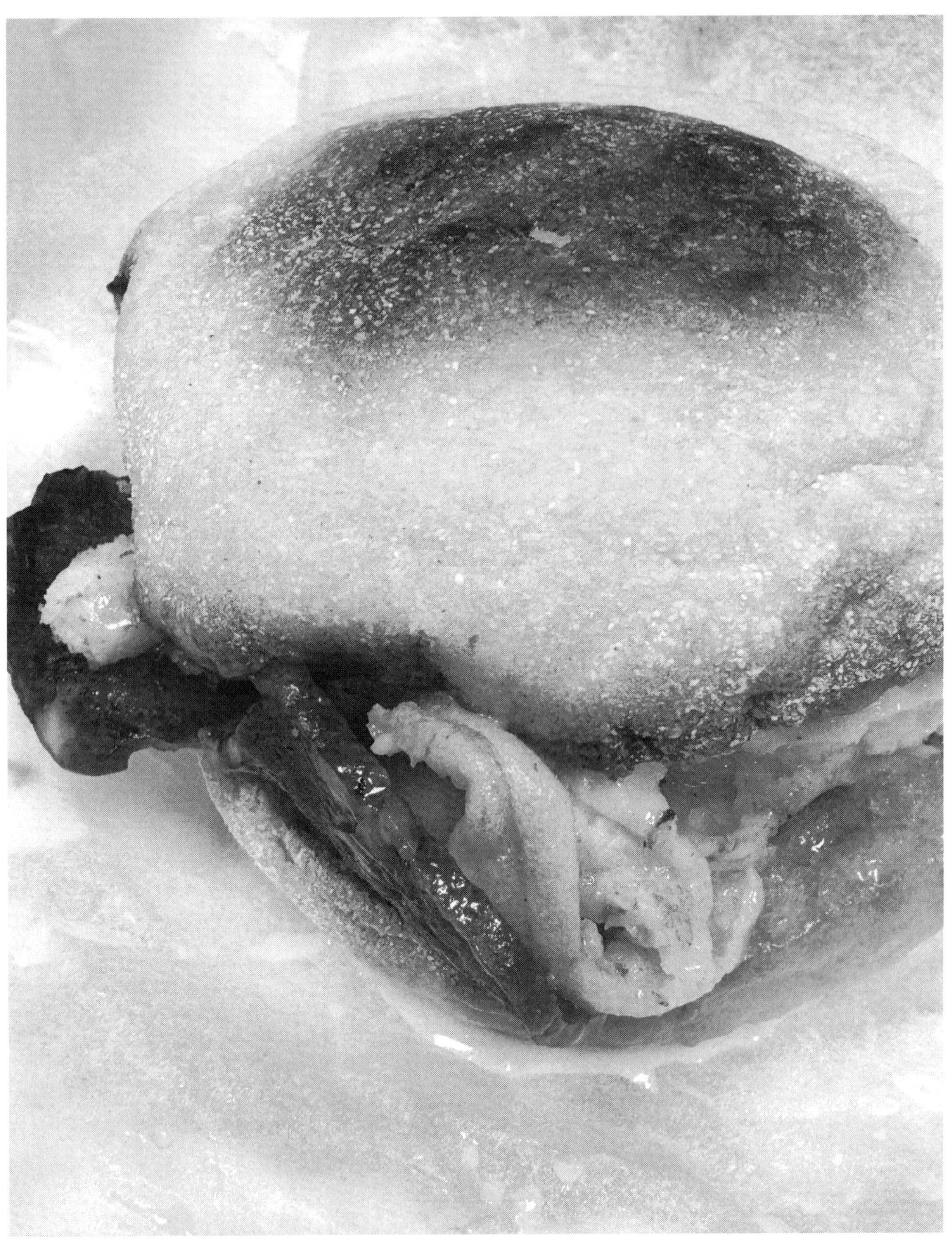

# FREEZER BREAKFAST SANDWICHES

**Serves 6**

## Ingredients

- 6 English muffins
- 12 eggs
- 1 1/2 cup cottage cheese
- 6 slices cheddar cheese
- 12 slices turkey bacon
- 1 tsp Pully Wissle P-DuB Rub
- dash Dried parsley
- dash Garlic powder

## Tools/Equipment Needed

- Dry/Plunger measuring cup
- Toaster or Air Fryer
- Blender or Immersion blender
- Large skillet
- Mini waffle maker (optional)

Toast English muffins in your toaster or try your air fryer! In a blender (or with an immersion blender), combine eggs, cottage cheese, and seasonings.

Cook turkey bacon over medium heat until crispy and browned on both sides. Remove from heat.

Cook eggs and top with cheddar slices. This is where that mini waffle maker can come in handy or use a mold to make your eggs sandwich size if you have one.

Place on toasted English muffins, add bacon, wrap in parchment paper, and store in a freezer bag or airtight container. They'll keep in the refrigerator for up to five days.

To reheat, microwave for 2 minutes and then place in the air fryer for 2 additional minutes. If freezing the sandwiches, I would recommend thaw in the refrigerator overnight.

# POWER MUESLI

From *Run Fast, Cook Fast, Eat Slow* by Shalane Flanagan and Elyse Kopecky

---

## Ingredients

- 4 cups old-fashioned rolled oats
- 1 cup walnuts, almonds, pecans, cashews, chopped
- 1/2 cup dried fruit (date pieces, chopped apricots, goji berries, raisins, etc.)
- 1/3 cup pumpkin seeds or sunflower seeds
- 1/3 cup unsweetened coconut flakes
- 1/4 cup sesame seeds or ground flax
- 1 Tbsp ground cinnamon

---

## Tools/Equipment Needed

- Dry measuring cups
- Measuring spoons
- Liquid measuring cups (when preparing to serve)

---

Uses for muesli: Store in a large glass or airtight container. This can be used to make both cold and hot oatmeal options. Already packed full of flavor, fiber, and nutrients, I recommend adding a scoop of protein powder to make this even more satiating for longer.

Overnight oats: In a cereal bowl, combine 1/2 cup muesli, 1/2 cup whole milk yogurt, and 1/3 cup unsweetened almond milk. Cover and allow it to sit in the fridge overnight.

Optional: Top with honey and fresh fruit.

Hot oatmeal: In a medium pot, bring 2 1/2 cups of liquid to a boil (1/2 water and 1/2 milk of choice is a great option). Add 1 1/2 cups of muesli and a pinch of salt. Reduce heat to low, cover, and simmer, stirring occasionally until the oatmeal thickens, about 10 minutes. Divide into two bowls and, optionally, add more milk to taste, drizzle with honey or molasses, and top with fresh fruit.

# PROTEIN PANCAKES

**Serves: 6**

### Ingredients

- 3 cups (246 g) old-fashioned rolled oats
- 3 cup (678 g) cottage cheese
- 12 large eggs
- 2 Tbsp maple syrup
- 2 Tbsp ground cinnamon
- 1 Tbsp vanilla extract
- 1 Tbsp salt
- 7 1/2 cup (1050 g) mixed berries

### Tools/Equipment Needed

- Dry measuring cups
- Plunger measuring cup (optional)
- Measuring spoons
- Blender
- Large skillet
- Rubber spatula
- Spatula
- Saucepan if making a compote with berries

Blend oatmeal, egg, cottage cheese, cinnamon, salt, vanilla, and sweetener in a blender.

Spray a pan over medium heat with non-stick spray.

Pour 1/4 cup of batter into the pan and cook for about 2 minutes or until lightly brown.

**Option 1:** You can add some of the berries to your pancakes while the first side is cooking. Just keep them away from the edges. Flip and cook the other side.

**Option 2:** Cook the pancakes plain and top with fresh berries. When reheated, the berries will "pop" and release their natural juices and sweetness, creating a "syrup."

**Option 3:** Cook the pancakes plain and place mixed berries in a saucepan with about a half-inch of water. Let them simmer to release their juice and sweetness. Top pancakes with berry compote when reheating and serving in place of a syrup.

Pure Maple Sy
BRENNEMAN
MAPLE
ONE PINT

# KETO PANCAKES

**Serves: 6**

## Ingredients

- 1/2 cup milk of choice
- 6 large eggs
- 2 Tbsp honey, maple syrup, or 10 drops liquid stevia
- 2 Tbsp coconut oil or lard, melted
- 3 cups almond flour
- 1 tsp vanilla
- 1/2 tsp salt
- 1 tsp baking soda
- 1/2 tsp apple cider vinegar

## Tools/Equipment Needed

- Liquid measuring cups
- Measuring spoons
- Dry measuring cups
- Blender or food processor
- Large skillet
- Rubber spatula
- spatula

Put all ingredients into a blender or food processor to bring it all together. Fry at medium heat with a bit of coconut oil or butter.

They are softer pancakes, so I fry them on a lower setting to allow more of them to set before they get too dark. These are great topped with a bit of nut butter, berries, and maple syrup.

# CHOCOLATE KETO WAFFLES

**Serves: 6**

## Ingredients

- 1 1/2 cup almond flour, not blanched
- 6 eggs
- 2 Tbsp stevia
- 1 Tbsp baking powder
- 6 Tbsp butter or lard, melted
- 1/2 to 1/3 cup milk of choice (may not need as much)
- 6 Tbsp cocoa powder
- Pinch of salt

## Tools/Equipment Needed

- Mixing bowl
- Dry measuring cups
- Measuring spoons
- Liquid measuring cup
- Waffle iron

In a bowl, combine all ingredients and stir until batter is formed. You may not need all the milk, so I saved that for last and added just enough to make a slightly loose batter.

Grease a hot waffle maker with non-stick spray. Pour in roughly 3-4 tablespoons of batter, close the lid, and cook for about 90 seconds or until cooked through. It doesn't take long!

10

# TURKEY BACON EGG BAKE WITH POTATOES

**Serves: 6-8**

### Ingredients

- 2 1-lb. packages of The Little Potato Co' A Little Garlic and Parsley
- 8 oz. button mushrooms, sliced
- 12 oz. package turkey bacon
- 1 medium-small onion
- 1 bell pepper
- 1 dozen eggs
- 2 cups egg whites
- 2 Tbsp olive oil
- 2 tsp Pully Wissle P-DuB Rub
- To taste: garlic powder, dried parsley
- 2 cups shredded mozzarella cheese

### Tools/Equipment Needed

- Cutting board
- Chef's knife
- Rimmed baking sheet
- Liquid measuring cup
- Measuring spoons
- Large skillet

Start by cutting the little potatoes into halves or quarters to your preference and preheating the oven to 450°F. Wipe any dirt off your mushrooms and cut into chunks. Peel and cut your onion(s) and peppers into large chunks. Toss these into a bowl with the olive oil and spices, including the spices from the Little Potato Co.

Coat everything evenly, then spread onto a cookie sheet pan (with a rim). Place in the oven and allow to roast until desired color and crispness. (I like mine pretty toasty, so I think it takes at least 30 minutes, and I turn it one or two times.)

While the potatoes are roasting, cut up your turkey bacon and cook in a large skillet until desired color. Turn off the heat, and once your potatoes are done, toss them into the skillet. Turn your oven to 325°F. Whisk the eggs and egg whites together and dump into the skillet. Bake until done all the way through, approximately 30 minutes. Top with cheese when you pull it out and allow it to melt while it cools. Cut into 6-8 equal pieces.

Note: You can swap out or omit the cheese to reduce calories and fats. Also, I didn't initially intend to use all 2 lbs. of potatoes, but the carb amount is actually good for me. You can adjust according to your needs and likes.

# COTTAGE CHEESE TOAST

**Serves: 1**

---

### Ingredients

- 1 slice whole grain bread
- 1/2 cup (113g) cottage cheese
- 1 Tbsp honey
- 1/4 tsp ground cinnamon

---

### Tools/Equipment Needed

- Toaster
- Plunger measuring cup
- Measuring spoons

---

Toast the slice of bread, top with cottage cheese, drizzle with honey, and sprinkle cinnamon.

Options: I like to top with fresh berries or make it savory with fresh sliced tomato, basil, and balsamic glaze.

For meal prep: Keep the toast in a separate container from the toppings. Top the toast when you're ready to eat.

# CROCK-POT BREAKFAST CASSEROLE

**Serves: 12**

### Ingredients

- 1 medium onion, diced
- 1 medium bell pepper, diced
- 16 oz. egg whites
- 12 large eggs
- 1 cup whole milk
- 18 oz. frozen hash brown potatoes (or grated fresh potatoes)
- Seasonings: Pully Wissle P-DuB Rub, dried parsley, garlic powder
- 2 cups shredded cheese
- 3 oz. cooked, crumbled bacon
- 12 turkey sausage patties (Jimmy Dean precooked)
- Maple syrup (optional topping)

### Tools/Equipment Needed

- Crock-Pot
- Cutting board
- Chef's knife
- Liquid measuring cup
- Dry measuring cup
- Large skillet
- Whisk
- Wooden spoon or rubber spatula

Spray your Crock-Pot with non-stick spray.

In a skillet, cook onion and bell pepper until softened (I like some color on mine). Meanwhile, whisk together eggs, egg whites, cheese, milk, and seasoning (to taste) in the Crock-Pot. You can cut up the sausage patties and add them or keep them as a side when the eggs (as shown).

When onion and pepper mix is done, add that to the Crock-Pot and snap on the lid.

Cook on high 3-4 hours or low 6-8 hours, depending on what you have going on that day.

Once the eggs are set, they're done. You may see some liquid at the top due to condensation from the steam being trapped. That's OK! Portion into containers with sausage patties and drizzle maple syrup before eating.

Note: Any extra servings can be frozen!

# MY GRANOLA FAVES

I have to admit, I'm a sucker for good granola on my homemade yogurt, along with some fruit. The crunchiness with the smooth and creamy yogurt—nothing compares. I have a few recipes that are my go-tos, and I want to share them with you.

---

### Gwendolyn's Peanut Butter Granola

- 4 1/2 cups old-fashioned rolled oats
- 1 cup Einkorn flour
- 1 tsp baking soda
- 2 tsp vanilla extract
- 2/3 cup olive oil
- 2/3 cup peanut butter
- 1/2 cup brown sugar

---

### Tools/Equipment Needed

- Dry measuring cups
- Measuring spoons
- Liquid measuring cup
- Plunger measuring cup
- Rimmed baking sheet
- Wooden spoon
- Spatula
- Oven

---

Preheat the oven to 325°F. Combine all ingredients in a large mixing bowl and spread onto a rimmed baking sheet. Bake, stirring every 15 minutes until toasted and golden.

# HONEY CARDAMOM GRANOLA

Adapted from *Run Fast, Cook Fast, Eat Slow* by Shalane Flanagan and Elyse Kopecky

## Ingredients

- 3 cups old-fashioned rolled oats
- 1/2 cup chopped walnuts
- 1/2 cup unsweetened coconut flakes
- 1 tsp ground cinnamon
- 1/2 tsp ground cardamom
- 1/2 tsp ground ginger
- 1/2 tsp sea salt
- 1/3 cup honey
- 1/3 cup extra virgin olive oil
- 1 tsp vanilla extract

## Tools/Equipment Needed

- Dry measuring cups
- Measuring spoons
- Liquid measuring cups
- Rimmed baking sheet
- Mixing bowl
- Spatula
- Wooden spoon or rubber spatula
- Oven

Preheat the oven to 325°F. Combine the ingredients and mix until well mixed. Spread out onto a rimmed baking sheet. Bake for about 40 minutes, stirring every 15-20 minutes.

# PISTACHIO AND PUMPKIN SEED GRANOLA

## Ingredients

- 3 cups old-fashioned rolled oats
- 1 1/2 cups pistachios
- 1 cup pumpkin seeds
- 1 cup unsweetened dried coconut flakes
- 1/2 cup maple syrup
- 1/2 cup extra virgin olive oil
- 1/2 cup light brown sugar
- 1 tsp kosher salt
- 1 tsp vanilla extract

## Tools/Equipment Needed

- Dry measuring cups
- Liquid measuring cups
- Measuring spoons
- Mixing bowl
- Wooden spoon or rubber spatula
- Rimmed baking sheet
- Spatula
- Oven

Preheat the oven to 325°F. Stir all of the ingredients together and mix well. Spread on a rimmed baking sheet. Stir every 15 minutes until granola is toasted and golden. Bake approximately 30 minutes.

# SNACK ATTACK

---

These are my favorite go-to snacks throughout the day, depending on my mood and current goals. (Can you tell I have a sweet tooth?)

---

- Greek yogurt with fresh berries and homemade granola . . . . . page 25 & 43
- Cheese and homemade herbed sourdough crackers
- Protein coffee . . . . page 95
- Protein mug cake . . . . page 37
- Mini Charcuterie Box . . . . page 39
- Watermelon Feta Salad
- Chocolate Truffle Bites . . . . page 47
- Hummus and veggies
- Yogurt and/or Cottage Cheese Dips (sweet and Savory) . . . . page 41-45
- Banana Peanut Butter Brownies . . . . page 35

---

Just because you're following a healthier lifestyle doesn't mean it's devoid of snacks and sweets. Life is about balance, and I have healthier options to satisfy your sweet tooth!

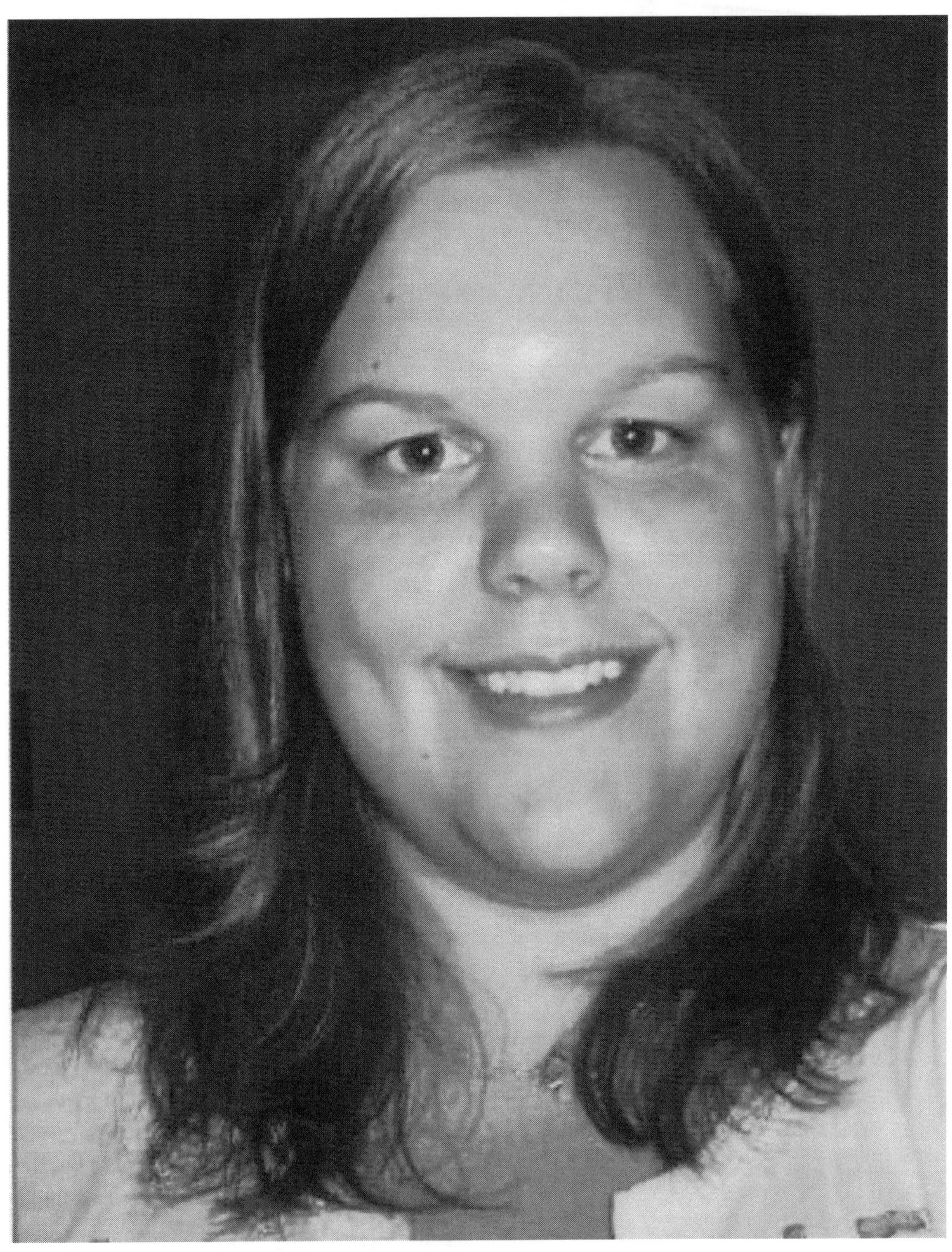

I went off to The Culinary Institute of America after high school, and during orientation, my tour guide mentioned, "Many colleges are known for the Freshman 15. We're known for the Freshman 45." With all the kitchen classes serving as their fellow students' dining options, there was a plethora of good food at our disposal. I remember thinking, "Oh God, I can't afford another forty-five pounds."

Well, social anxiety kept me from many of the dining opportunities at school for a good portion of that first year. I often went back to my room to eat Ramen noodles in solitude, giving in to my social anxiety. I also started to drink water. Yes, water. At home, I drank soda and milk all the time and rarely drank any water. I would get such charlie horses at night. Now, in college, if I wanted soda, I had to buy it, and I definitely could not afford to buy soda.

Throughout my externship, between my freshman and sophomore years, I had such nerves and anxiety that I could barely eat. I'd have half a bagel before work and typically eat until a family meal (on a long shift and only because my coworkers made me stop to eat) or until my shift was done and I was back at the apartment. Eating so little and working all the time added up to losing thirty pounds that summer, and I went back to school watching how my peers would eat. If they didn't finish their plates, neither did I. What they ordered, I ordered. They were smaller than me, so it made sense that I followed what they were doing. And it was working—for a while.

# BANANA PEANUT BUTTER BROWNIES

**Serves: 8**

## Ingredients

- 1 1/2 bananas, mashed
- 1/2 cup peanut butter (look for one that's made with nuts and salt only)
- 1/4 cup cocoa powder
- 1/2 cup peanut butter-flavored protein powder

## Tools/Equipment Needed

- Medium mixing bowl
- Fork or potato masher
- Wooden spoon or rubber spatula
- 8x8 baking pan
- Parchment paper
- Oven
- Chef's knife

Preheat oven to 350°F. Combine all ingredients, stirring well. Pour into a buttered or parchment-lined 8x8-inch baking pan. Bake for 12-15 minutes until the center is just set. Allow to cool completely before using a chef's knife to cut into 16 pieces.

LIFE'S
TOO SHORT
to the

# PROTEIN MUG CAKE

**Serves: 1**

---

## Ingredients

- 1/4 cup all-purpose flour
- 1 scoop protein powder
- 1 Tbsp organic cane sugar
- 1/4 tsp baking powder
- 1/4 tsp cinnamon
- 1/8 tsp allspice
- 3 Tbsp half-and-half
- 1 Tbsp butter
- 1/4 tsp vanilla extract

---

## Optional toppings:

- Whipped cream
- 1 Tbsp chocolate chips
- 1 Tbsp maple syrup

---

## Tools/Equipment Needed

- Dry measuring cup
- Measuring spoons
- 12-oz. mug
- Microwave

---

In a 12-ounce mug, melt the butter. Stir in remaining ingredients until well combined. Microwave 60 seconds. Add one or two of the toppings, if desired.

# SNACK "BOXES" / MINI CHARCUTERIE BOX

**Serves: 6**

---

### Ingredients

- 3 oz. oven-roasted turkey deli meat
- 3 oz. hard salami
- 6 oz. aged cheddar cheese
- 30 whole-grain crackers
- 60 red seedless grapes
- 12 mini snacking peppers, optional

---

### Tools/Equipment Needed

- Food scale
- Cutting board
- Chef's knife
- Meal prep containers

---

The key with charcuterie boards is to have two different kinds of meat, one on the fatty side and one leaner, and add fiber with fruit and veggies. Charcuterie boards are so tasty because they have a mix of textures, salty and sweet. Feel free to make comparable substitutions to your liking!

# COTTAGE CHEESE AND VEGGIES

**Serves: 1**

---

### Ingredients

- 1 cup cottage cheese
- Veggies of choice: cucumbers, radishes, snacking peppers, carrots, jicama, zucchini, etc.

---

### Tools/Equipment Needed

- Cutting board
- Chef's knife or mandolin
- Dry or plunger measuring cup
- Wooden spoon or rubber spatula if adding herbs/seasoning to the cottage cheese

---

Carefully slice veggies with a knife or mandolin.
Portion the cottage cheese. Add fresh or dried herbs, garlic, or ranch dressing mix for extra flavor.

# YOGURT

Plain Greek yogurt has been a very versatile staple for me for years. Typically, I use it as a snack with fruit and sometimes homemade granola. It can also be made into a fruit dip, used as a replacement for sour cream, or even made savory for veggies and crackers. It's higher in protein than traditional-style yogurt and has a thicker consistency. I choose plain to control the added ingredients, including the sugar or sweetener content. Often, all it needs is some good fruit and a small drizzle of honey or vanilla.

# HIGH-PROTEIN FRUIT DIP

**Serves: 1**

## Ingredients

- 170g plain Greek yogurt
- 1 scoop peanut butter-flavored protein powder
- 1 apple, sliced
- Dash cinnamon

## Tools/Equipment Needed

- Cutting board
- Chef's or paring knife
- Food scale
- Small bowl

Mix yogurt and protein powder. Top with a dash of cinnamon.

# PROTEIN CHOCOLATE TRUFFLES

**Serves: 12-14**

## Ingredients

- 1 15-oz. can chickpeas, drained and rinsed
- 3/4 cup dark cocoa powder
- 1/2 cup maple syrup
- 1/3 cup peanut butter
- 1 tsp vanilla extract
- 1/2 tsp salt
- 2 scoops peanut butter protein powder
- 1 cup dark chocolate coating wafers (such as Merkens or Lindt)

## Tools/Equipment Needed

- Food processor
- Can opener
- Dry measuring cup
- Plunger measuring cup
- Measuring spoons
- Small, microwave-safe bowl
- Spoon or small cookie scoop

Use a food processor to blend chickpeas, cocoa powder, maple syrup, peanut butter, vanilla, salt, and protein powder. Using a small cookie scoop, portion truffle balls onto a parchment-lined cookie sheet. Place it in the freezer to set it up for about 20 minutes.

In the microwave or over a double boiler, carefully melt the chocolate. If doing this in the microwave, stir well every 20-30 seconds until completely melted and smooth. It should not take long, and you shouldn't overheat the chocolate. It can burn easily and seize up.

Remove truffles from the freezer, and using a fork, coat each one. This takes some practice! Place back on the parchment paper and allow the chocolate to set. Store in the fridge for up to five days.

# ROASTED BEET AND COTTAGE CHEESE BOWL

**Serves: 6**

## Ingredients

- 565g red and/or golden beets
- 640g carrots, chopped
- 5 tsp olive oil
- Salt and pepper to taste
- 2 Tbsp minced garlic
- 5 Tbsp lemon juice
- 15 tsp fresh rosemary
- 1700g cottage cheese
- 10 Tbsp shelled pistachios, salted

## Tools/Equipment Needed

- Food scale
- Cutting board
- Chef's knife
- Measuring spoons
- 1 medium mixing bowl
- 1 large mixing bowl
- Rimmed baking sheet

Preheat oven to 450°F. Peel and chop beets and carrots into small chunks. Toss together with olive oil, salt, and pepper. Place on a rimmed baking sheet and roast until fork tender and starting to caramelize. This should take about bout 40 minutes.

Stir together cottage cheese, garlic, lemon juice, and rosemary with salt and pepper to taste. Serve the cottage cheese in a bowl topped with veggies and pistachios.

# LUNCHES AND DINNERS

I never learned much about food, what it does to and for the body, how to manage it, and why I couldn't seem to grasp it. Why were some people capable of feeling satisfied on less? Were they actually satisfied? All I knew was that some things were "good," some were "bad," and too much overall would make me gain weight.

By the time I left college, spent some time in California, and returned home, I was down about eighty pounds. I was used to working out and not eating much, but now that I was back in my parents' home, food was not in short supply. I was also paying off college debt, so a gym membership was not in the cards for me. I needed that time to make money. When a college friend of mine moved in with us, she convinced me to join her at the gym and we made it work for a while. I was approached by a trainer and signed up for three months. I saw incredible results with him, and I started doing things I didn't know I was capable of. We still never really talked about nutrition. When I stopped training with him because he was leaving the gym and I didn't want to continue with his replacement, he said, "You're not going to keep your results without a trainer."

I wanted to prove him wrong, but he was right. It wasn't immediate, but I eventually fell back on the bad habits and the weight returned with it. I wasn't eating as many vegetables and fruits. I was just about making life easy and eating what my family ate. My college friend moved cross country, so I no longer had a gym or food accountability partner. I was also going through some emotional stuff that I couldn't even consciously recognize. Before too long, I got swept back up into alcohol and food to cope with how life was going, and though the scale didn't reach my original weight, I looked heavier than ever before.

# BEEF AND BROCCOLI

**Serves: 6**

## Ingredients

- 3 Tbsp corn starch
- 36 oz. round top steak, thinly sliced
- 1 1/2 Tbsp fresh ginger, grated
- 1 1/2 Tbsp brown sugar
- 1 1/2 Tbsp garlic clove, minced
- 1 1/8 cup soy sauce
- 1 medium onion, chopped
- 2 1/2 cups cooked rice
- 3 Tbsp sesame seeds
- 9 cups broccoli florets
- 3 1/2 Tbsp olive oil

## Tools/Equipment Needed

- Measuring spoons
- Cutting board
- Chef's knife
- Liquid measuring cup
- Dry measuring cups
- Whisk
- Small mixing bowl
- Medium mixing bowl
- Large skillet
- Saucepan or rice cooker

Whisk 2 tablespoons of cornstarch with 3 tablespoons of water. Toss in beef slices. In a separate bowl, whisk 1 tablespoon of cornstarch with soy sauce, brown sugar, garlic, and grated ginger. In a skillet, heat 1 tablespoon of oil. Add beef slices and cook until almost done. Set aside. Add remaining oil to the pan, heat, and add broccoli florets and sliced onions, cooking until tender. Return beef to the pan and add prepared sauce. Bring to a boil and cook for 1 minute. Serve over rice and sprinkle with sesame seeds.

# TURKEY MEATBALLS

**Serves: 6**

## Ingredients

- 3 lbs. lean ground turkey
- 10 oz. frozen spinach, thawed and drained
- 1 cup grated parmesan
- 2 large eggs
- Salt, pepper, dried basil, parsley, Italian seasoning, and garlic powder to taste

## Tools/Equipment Needed

- Large mixing bowl
- .75 to 1-ounce cookie scoop
- Rimmed baking sheet
- Wooden spoon
- Colander
- Parchment paper

Combine all ingredients in a large mixing bowl. Use a cookie scoop for evenly sized meatballs (I use a purple-handled one). Place on a parchment-lined sheet tray in a 425°F oven and bake until golden brown and bubbly. Serve this with pasta, zucchini noodles, or some sauteed veggies of your choosing.

# SALMON POKE BOWL

**Serves: 6**

### Ingredients

- 14 oz. broth of choice (I typically use chicken)
- 1 cup brown rice
- 1 bag (12-16 oz.) frozen cauliflower rice
- 3 spring onions
- 1/2 Tbsp fresh grated ginger
- 2 Tbsp sesame oil
- 1 Tbsp minced garlic
- 1 cup liquid aminos
- 1 1/2 lbs. salmon, raw
- 1 large red bell pepper (2 cups chopped)
- 1 Tbsp honey
- 6 medium cucumbers
- 6 tsp sesame seeds
- 1 1/2 avocado, sliced

### Tools/Equipment Needed

- Can opener
- Dry measuring cup
- Measuring spoons
- Liquid measuring cup
- Cutting board
- Chef's knife
- 2-quart saucepan with lid
- Large mixing bowl
- Whisk
- Vegetable peeler
- Spoon
- Large skillet

In a 2-quart saucepan, bring broth to a boil. Add dry brown rice, cover with lid, reduce the heat to a simmer, and cook until all liquid is absorbed.

Remove from heat and stir in cauliflower rice. While that's cooling, whisk together spring onion, grated ginger, sesame oil, garlic, and liquid aminos in a bowl. Cut salmon into 6 portions and place into a bowl. Allow to marinate 5 minutes or up to 2 hours.

Meanwhile, chop the red bell pepper and set aside. Also, peel the cucumbers. Slice in half lengthwise, scoop out the seeds, and chop into 1/2" to 3/4" pieces; set those aside.

Heat a skillet on medium and coat the pan with non-stick spray or lard. Place salmon portions skin side down in a pan and allow to cook 2-3 minutes on each side or to your liking. When salmon is done, remove from the pan and add red bell pepper.

Whisk honey into the remaining marinade and add to the pan as well. Let that simmer for 1-2 minutes. If it simmers too long, it will reduce and become even saltier. Portion your rice into containers, top with chopped cucumber, avocado, salmon portions, and bell pepper, and sprinkle sesame seeds on the top.

# ROASTED VEGETABLE KALE SALAD WITH PORK LOIN

**Serves: 6**

## Ingredients

- 3 Tbsp honey
- 4 1/2 Tbsp olive oil, divided
- 2 lbs. red and/or golden beets
- 12 large carrots
- 2 medium onions
- 12-ounce package baby bella mushrooms
- 2 tsp Pully Wissle P-DuB Rub, divided
- 2 Tbsp ranch dressing mix
- 1/2 Tbsp dried parsley
- 2 tsp garlic powder
- Pinch of salt and coarse black pepper
- 2 lbs. boneless pork loin
- 12 cups chopped kale

## Tools/Equipment Needed

- Measuring spoons
- Cutting board
- Chef's knife
- Large mixing bowl
- Rimmed baking sheet
- Instant pot or slow cooker

Preheat the oven to 450°F. Peel and chop beets, carrots, and onions. Place all into a large mixing bowl. Wipe mushrooms, cut in half or quarters, and add to the bowl. Toss with 3 tablespoons olive oil and P-DuB Rub. Place on a rimmed baking sheet and roast for 30-45 minutes or until desired color and doneness are reached.

Season pork with ranch dressing mix, dried parsley, garlic powder, salt, and coarse black pepper. Place in an Instant Pot on the slow cooker setting, or use a slow cooker for about 3 1/2 to 4 hours until internal temperature reaches 165°F. Sort through kale, remove the stem pieces, and chop any large pieces. Place into a large mixing bowl. Massage with a drizzle of lemon juice and 1 teaspoon P-DuB Rub to help tenderize the leaves. Divide kale into meal prep containers. Top with roasted vegetables and sliced pork loin.

# PIZZA CHICKEN

**Serves: 6**

### Ingredients

- 1lb., 8oz. chicken breast
- 13 oz. tomato sauce
- Italian seasoning Garlic Powder Pully Wissle P-DuB Rub
- 8 oz. mozzarella
- Pepperoni (optional)

### Tools/Equipment Needed

- Cutting board
- Chef's knife
- Large cast iron skillet
- Aluminum foil

Portion chicken breast into 4–5-ounce pieces and season with P-DuB, Italian seasoning, and garlic powder over the top and rub all over. Cook in the cast iron skillet on all sides until almost cooked through.

Top with tomato sauce, mozzarella cheese, and pepperoni (if using). Cover with foil and place into a preheated 200°F oven to melt the cheese.

# BIG MAC SALAD

**Serves: 4**

## Ingredients

- 1 lb. lean ground sirloin
- 1 medium onion, diced
- 1 small bell pepper, diced
- 2 Tbsp prepared yellow mustard
- 2 Tbsp dill pickle juice
- 1 cup shredded cheddar cheese
- 1/2 cup Thousand Island dressing
- 2 medium Roma tomatoes, diced
- 4 dill pickle spears, diced
- 2 Tbsp ketchup
- 4 Tbsp sesame seeds
- 16 oz. lettuce, fresh or shredded and bagged

## Tools/Equipment Needed

- Cutting board
- Chef's knife
- Large skillet
- Colander
- Measuring spoons

In a skillet, brown beef with onions, peppers, mustard, and pickle juice until beef is done and onions are translucent. Drain mixture and add in cheese, Thousand Island dressing, and tomatoes.

If you're serving this immediately, throw it all together, topping the salad with ketchup and a sprinkle of sesame seeds. But if you intend to prepare it ahead of time, store salad mix and meat mixture separately. You can use a jar by putting the meat mixture, pickles, and ketchup in first. Then top with lettuce and sesame seeds.

# CRUNCHY ORANGE CHICKEN SALAD

**Serves: 6**

### Ingredients

- 1 head Romaine lettuce, chopped
- 8 oz. bag spring mix greens
- 1/2 cup chopped scallions/green onions
- 2 large carrots, grated
- 3 1/2 lbs. chicken, breast or thighs
- 6 mandarin oranges
- 3 oz. chow mein noodles
- 6 Tbsp sliced almonds or sunflower seeds

### Dressing:

- 1 1/2 tsp sesame oil
- 4 1/2 Tbsp rice vinegar
- 2 1/2 Tbsp honey
- 1 1/2 Tbsp hoisin sauce
- 3 Tbsp soy sauce
- 3/4 Tbsp fresh ginger, minced or grated
- 2 1/4 Tbsp vegetable oil
- 2 cloves garlic

### Tools/Equipment Needed

- Cutting board
- Chef's knife
- Grater
- Skillet
- Measuring spoons
- Blender/immersion blender
- Large mixing bowl

Cook chicken in a skillet until thoroughly cooked. Then shred or chop.

Toss the lettuce, spring mix, green onions, and carrots together in a large bowl and portion into meal prep containers. Portion out chicken on the side or in a separate container so as not to make the greens wilty.

Peel and segment the oranges and add to the chicken. Chow mein noodles and almonds can also be kept separate since they do not need to be refrigerated. You can also place them on top of greens.

Combine all the dressing ingredients in a blender or use an immersion blender to thoroughly combine. Dress salad before serving.

# BEEF BULGOGI

**Serves: 6**

## Ingredients

- 16 oz. beef flank steak
- 2 Tbsp soy sauce
- 1 Tbsp ginger root raw
- 1 Tbsp brown sugar
- 1/2 Tbsp sesame oil
- 1 clove garlic raw
- 1 tsp crushed red pepper flakes
- 1 tsp olive oil or lard
- 4 large eggs
- 1 small (3 inches long) green onions or scallions
- 1 small (6 3/8 inches long) cucumber, peeled raw
- 2 cup (300g) Kimchi
- 2 cups cooked rice
- 4 Tbsp sesame seeds

## Tools/Equipment Needed

- Medium mixing bowl
- Cutting board
- Chef's knife
- Large skillet
- Vegetable peeler
- Spoon
- Saucepan or rice cooker
- Measuring spoons
- Food scale
- Dry measuring cup

Start by slicing steak into thin strips and placing it in a bowl to marinate with crushed garlic, soy sauce, pepper flakes, ginger, sugar, and sesame oil. After 10-15 minutes, add the marinated beef to a preheated skillet over medium-high heat with olive oil or lard. Cook in a single layer until browned, cooked, and crisp at the edges. Season lightly with salt and pepper.

For the cucumbers, use a vegetable peeler to make ribbons or dice. If dicing, remove the seeds after cutting in half lengthwise. Then cut to desired size. Remove and top steamed rice with beef, sliced green onion, kimchi, sesame seeds, fried egg, and cucumber.

# CHIPOTLE CHICKEN TACO MEAT

**Serves: 12**

## Ingredients

- 3 lbs. boneless skinless chicken breast
- 2 Tbsp Pully Wissle Provisions taco seasoning
- Chipotle chili powder
- Pink Himalayan Sea Salt
- Coarse black pepper
- 1 Tbsp lard or olive oil
- 1 medium red onion
- 1 medium bell pepper (any color)
- 1-2 jalapenos or hot peppers of choice
- 1 8-oz. can Chipotle pepper sauce
- 1 Tbsp minced garlic or 4 cloves fresh garlic
- 1 whole lime

## Tools/Equipment Needed

- Cutting board
- Chef's knife
- Can opener
- Food scale
- Measuring spoons
- Large skillet
- Tongs

Cut onion, bell pepper, and hot peppers. Heat fat in a skillet over medium heat. Add onion and peppers and start to sauté. Once they get a little soft on the edges, then add garlic until fragrant.

While that's working, season chicken breasts and add to the pan. Pour chipotle sauce over the top. Fill that can with hot water and add to the pan. Allow the mixture to come to a boil, reduce heat to low, and simmer until the chicken is fully cooked, flipping about halfway through cooking (about 15 minutes per side).

I covered them with foil when they were almost cooked through, turned off the heat, and allowed them to finish cooking and start cooling. Once the chicken is cool enough to handle, shred or cut it into chunks.

Serve on top of a salad, in taco shells with toppings of choice (ideas listed below) or with cilantro lime rice, beans, and veggies for a taco bowl. The choice is yours, and they're endless!

**Taco or taco bowl toppings:** salad greens, cilantro, pickled red onion, fresh or canned salsa, Pico de Gallo, plain Greek yogurt (in lieu of sour cream), fresh shredded Monterey jack, queso fresco, black beans, pickled jalapenos, lime wedges, cilantro lime rice

# RANCH CHICKEN AND ROASTED VEGETABLES

(Roasted Vegetables can be found on page 79.)

**Serves: 6**

## Ingredients

- 1 lb., 15 oz. boneless skinless chicken breast
- 3 Tbsp Ranch dressing mix
- 1 cup chicken bone broth or water

## Tools/Equipment Needed

- Food scale
- Measuring spoons
- Liquid measuring cup
- Instant pot

Toss the chicken with ranch dressing mix.

In Instant Pot, add water and the rack, then layer seasoned chicken on top.

Poultry → High pressure → Normal Temperature → Sealed → 8 minutes

Leave on low for 8 minutes and release the pressure (I never get the chicken out right away, so I try to factor that time in as well). Check to make sure the chicken is fully cooked.

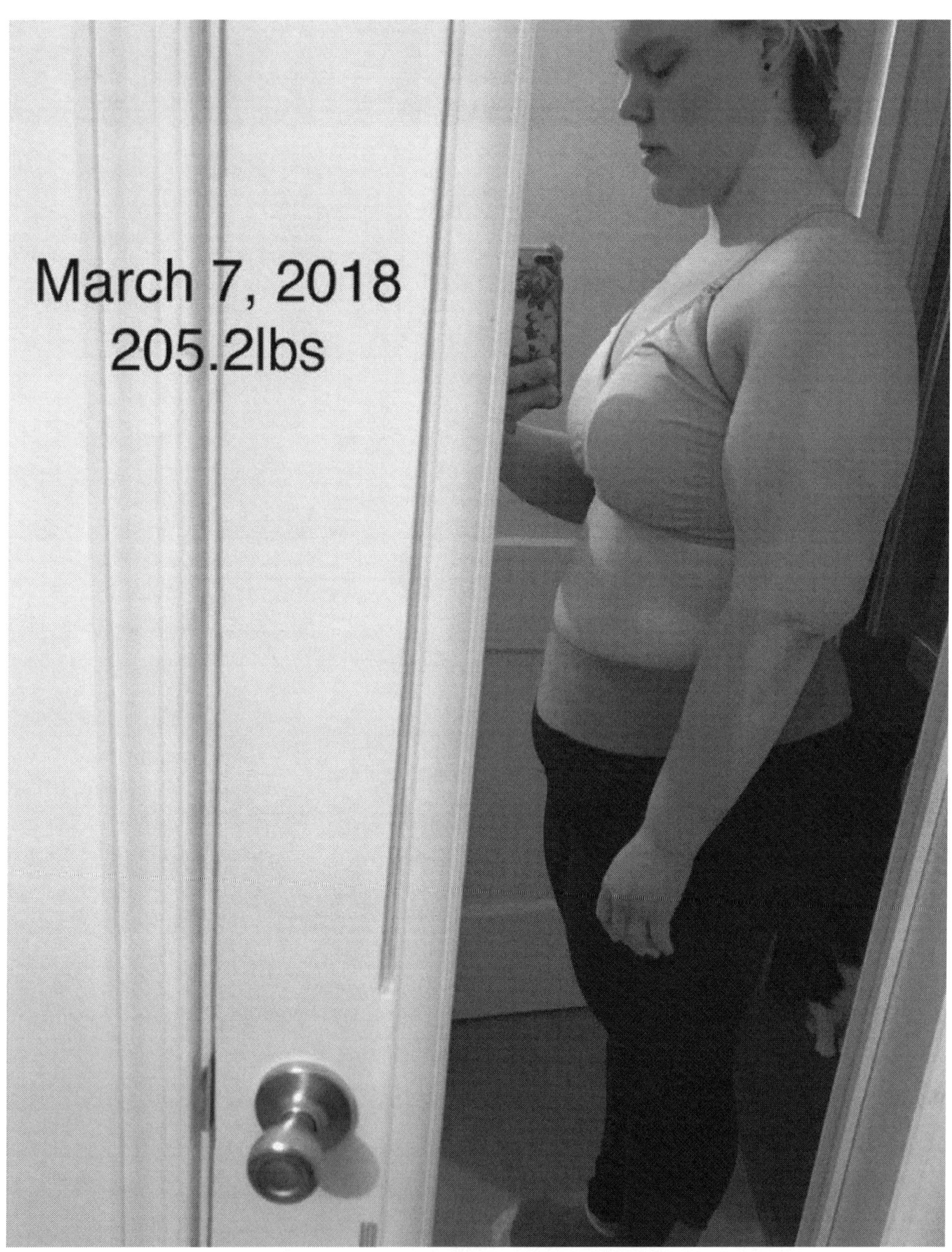
March 7, 2018
205.2lbs

# SIDES

I keep these relatively simple most of the time. I know what I like and what works for me.

Frozen veggies are a must. They're inexpensive, and you don't have to do anything to them but add some seasoning (unless you want them plain, that's OK too). I'll divide a bag or two of frozen vegetables among my containers, and that's it. When I heat up my meal, they'll be thawed out, and all they need is to be heated up. Add some salt, pepper, and garlic powder (or whatever you like), and they're good to go.

Rice, roasted potatoes, or sweet potatoes are my go-to side dishes, so I'm going to showcase them here.

When I moved out, in a way, it was a sigh of relief. I had my own space, and I could control what foods came in the door. I started to learn a little bit more about food and exercise. I was following an online program for their workouts and used the nutrition plan that coincided with it. Looking back now, with the knowledge that I've since gained, I wasn't eating enough of the right things even then. I was in a cycle of trying to be perfect and on plan, but I was still hungry. At that time, I was working in the food industry and still snacking all day (mostly on candy and sweets), trying to cope with stress. I'd then get upset with myself about not being perfect and, "Why can't I just follow this as it is?" that I'd snack more.

It still blows my mind that I lost weight like I did. That just indicates to me now that I wasn't getting enough protein and overall calories and wasn't in tune with my body enough to work on my relationship with food. The ups and downs of the scale would continue, even after I became a personal trainer myself, even to this day.

I became a personal trainer mainly to gain more knowledge. I was encouraged to become a personal trainer because I was already sharing my fitness journey online and trying to teach others how to get started and be successful. I had so much yet to learn, and I suppose I always will. I worked with other coaches to help me lose body fat (not just weight) and understand reverse dieting so that I could fuel myself (properly) to gain muscle and not continue trying to live off a low-calorie "diet" that was keeping in a never-ending rollercoaster of restrict-binge (most of you know what I'm talking about).

It was not a linear process.—I repeat, it was *not* a linear process. I was so inaccurate in tracking my food when I was in a deficit that when I attempted to reverse it, I would go way overboard and gain weight. I then sent myself into such a spiral of feeling like I'd failed and let my coach down that I didn't know how to come back. That spiral spilled into other areas of my life, and it was a deep, dark hole I had to dig myself out of. I am grateful that I haven't hit 200 pounds in a long time. For the most part, I've been able to maintain the same weight for the last year or two, but the mental aspect of that climb has been the hardest.

**Photo cred: AJ Norton**

# ROASTED VEGETABLES

**Serves: 6**

## Ingredients

- 1 lb., 8 oz. sweet potatoes, chunked
- 2 heads fresh broccoli, cut into florets about the size of sweet potatoes
- 1 large onion, cut into chunks
- 2 Tbsp olive oil
- 2 pinches of Pully Wissle P-DuB Rub
- 4 Tbsp ranch dressing mix

## Tools/Equipment Needed

- Food scale
- Cutting board
- Chef's knife
- Large mixing bowl
- Measuring spoons
- Rimmed baking sheet

Cut all the vegetables and toss with the remaining ingredients. Spread out in a single layer on a rimmed baking sheet and roast at 450°F for about 30-45 minutes, depending upon how much color you prefer.

# BASIC RICE

**Serves: 6**

I don't own a rice cooker yet. I'm still doing this thing old-school with a saucepan.

## Ingredients

- 2 cups chicken broth
- 1 cup dry brown rice

## Tools/Equipment Needed

- Liquid measuring cup
- Dry measuring cup
- Saucepan with lid
- Fork

Bring broth to a boil. Add some salt if necessary. Pour in your rice and stir once. Cover with a lid and lower the heat to a simmer. Let the rice cook with the lid on top until all the liquid is absorbed. This will take 20-25 minutes. Use a fork to fluff up and divide into your containers.

# CILANTRO LIME RICE

**Serves: 6**

This is my favorite for any kind of taco dish. Serve it alongside tacos, in a burrito bowl, or over your taco salad. There's so much flavor!

---

## Ingredients

- 1 cup white rice
- 1 cup bone broth (chicken)
- 1 cup water
- 1 bunch cilantro
- 2 limes

---

## Tools/Equipment Needed

- Dry measuring cup
- Liquid measuring cup
- Saucepan with lid
- Citrus juicer/reamer
- Zester/Microplane
- Cutting board
- Chef's knife

---

In a saucepan, heat broth and water to a boil. Add rice, lower the heat to simmer, and cover. Allow the rice to simmer until fully cooked, about 20-30 minutes. While that's cooking, chop cilantro and zest and juice the limes. When the rice is done cooking, remove from heat and stir in the cilantro, lime zest, and juice. Makes 6-10 servings (depending upon your portion sizes)

*Want to add some extra tropical flavor?*

# COCONUT CILANTRO LIME RICE (FAVORITE)

**Serve: 6**

---

## Ingredients

- 1 cup white rice
- 1 can coconut milk and enough water to equal 2 cups liquid
- 1 bunch cilantro
- 2 limes

---

## Tools/Equipment Needed

- Dry measuring cup
- Liquid measuring cup
- Saucepan with lid
- Cutting board
- Chef's knife
- Microplane/zester

---

# ROASTED POTATOES OR SWEET POTATOES

**Serves: 6**

## Ingredients

- 1 1/2 lbs. potatoes
- 1 large onion
- 12 oz. button or baby bella mushrooms
- 2 Tbsp olive oil
- 2 tsp sea salt
- 1 tsp coarse black pepper
- 2 tsp chili powder
- 1 tsp paprika
- Pinch cayenne pepper to taste
- 1 Tbsp dried parsley

## Tools/Equipment Needed

- Food scale
- Cutting board
- Chef's knife
- Measuring spoons
- Rimmed baking sheet
- Large mixing bowl

Heat oven to 450°F. Wash potatoes and mushrooms and peel the onion. Chop everything into equal-sized pieces and combine in a bowl. Drizzle olive and add seasonings. Mix everything well until coated. Spread out onto a rimmed baking pan and roast until tender and crisp to your liking (about 40-50 minutes for me).

# CREAMY CAULIFLOWER MASHED POTATOES

**Serves: 6**

Thank you to Lexi Lehr for this recommendation! This is a great way to curb that craving for creamy mashed potatoes with less fat and some extra vegetables hidden.

---

### Ingredients

- 3-4 cloves roasted garlic (instructions to follow)
- 2 lbs. Yukon gold potatoes
- 1 lb. cauliflower florets (raw)
- 1 Tbsp minced rosemary
- 4-6 Tbsp olive oil or butter, plus extra oil to roast garlic
- Salt and pepper to taste
- Starchy water, if needed

### Tools/Equipment Needed

- Food scale
- Measuring spoons
- Aluminum foil
- Small baking dish
- Cutting board
- Chef's knife
- Kettle with lid
- Slotted spoon or "spider"
- Food processor
- Rubber spatula

---

Roasted garlic: Place a whole bulb of garlic onto a piece of foil and coat heavily with olive oil. Place in a 350°F oven for about 20 minutes until the garlic has softened. Allow to cool before handling. The cloves should squeeze right out of the bulb. Use what you need and store the remainder in the fridge.

Slice or chop potatoes. You can peel them if you prefer, but I leave the skins on.

Place in a kettle with cold water. Bring up to a boil, add salt, and then simmer until fork tender. Drain, keeping the water to cook the cauliflower. Place florets in the hot water and bring back to a simmer, allowing them to cook until tender. Drain while reserving the water, as you may need it later.

Place cooked cauliflower in a food processor until almost fully pureed, then add potatoes. Process on medium until combined. Add the seasonings as well as butter/olive oil. Check consistency, adding salt and pepper to your taste. If it's a little thick, add some of the starchy water.

This has become one of my favorite side dishes!

Free To Be

# BEVERAGES

Ball

# PROTEIN SMOOTHIES

**Serves: 1**

---

## Ingredients

- 1 medium frozen banana
- 200-250g frozen berries
- 1/2 to 1 cup milk (your choice)
- 1 scoop protein powder

---

## Tools/Equipment Needed

- Blender
- Liquid measuring cup
- Rubber spatula

---

Put all ingredients in a quality blender and blend on medium or high speed. You may need to scrape it down with a rubber spatula and run it a second time. It's a little on the thick side with 1/2 cup milk, so feel free to add more if it suits you! Use a rubber spatula to scrape all the goodness out of the blender cup.

This also makes for a good snack at the end of a summer day. I sometimes add my magnesium supplement to this when using it as a nighttime snack.

# COLLAGEN OR PROTEIN COFFEE

**Serves: 1**

I like to start my days with protein coffee. It's an easy way to get 15+ grams of protein to kick off the morning. Coffee, for me, is like a warm hug comforting me from the inside out. If you opt for a flavored protein like I do, the amounts can be adjusted depending on how sweet you like your coffee. Those who prefer black, unsweetened coffee can certainly opt for unflavored—no guarantees on the taste!

---

### Ingredients

- 4 cups brewed coffee
- 1/3 cup milk of choice (I exclusively use local raw milk)
- 1 scoop collagen or protein powder
- Whipped cream, such as Reddi Whip (optional)

### Tools/Equipment Needed

- Coffee pot
- Large mug
- Milk frothing wand
- Liquid measuring cup

---

I own a four-cup coffee pot that I brew every morning. It's the perfect amount for most mornings, and I am OK with this level of sweetness.

Measure the milk in a very large mug or a glass measuring cup and microwave for 30 seconds. I like to take the chill off the milk so it doesn't cool down my hot coffee. Add the collagen and use a milk frothing wand to incorporate. Pour into your mug and add your coffee.

It's recommended to blend with milk before adding the hot coffee so as not to "cook" the protein and form lumps. (Trust me, it's not tasty.)

You may need to stir it up or grab that frothing wand again to ensure it's fully incorporated. For those who like it less sweet, start with a half-scoop of Collagen. You can always add more, but you won't be able to take it out.

If making iced coffee, you'll still want to dissolve the protein powder into cold liquid, then add ice.

Note: You can use unflavored collagen coffee for no added flavor or sweetness yet still getting that protein boost to start the day.

LANT LADY
RESULTS
1st Phorm
App Download
Peach Ring
Unlock the freshness & enjoy!
Mint Medley®
HERBAL TEA
Blend of cool garden
spearmint & peppermint

# SLEEPY TIME TEA

**Serves: 1**

## Ingredients

- 1 mug of water
- 1 tea bag of choice (Opt for a green or herbal tea that doesn't contain caffeine. My favorites are Chamomile, Mint Medley, and Ginger Peach.)
- 1 scoop magnesium supplement, flavored or unflavored

## Tools/Equipment Needed

- Mug
- Milk frothing wand

Follow the directions on the bag of tea. Each one has a slightly different steeping time, and you want to ensure you get an appropriate amount of flavor without it getting bitter, as some do.

Once the steep time is through, use a frothing wand to mix in your scoop of magnesium. Enjoy, and sweet dreams!

1st
phorm

# Brand Recommendations

These are not sponsored in any way. These are brands that I either currently use or have used in the past and enjoyed. Feel free to experiment to find what you love!

- **Pully Wissle Provisions.** P-DuB Rub is an all-purpose seasoning. The taco seasoning is also a favorite.
- **1st Phorm.** Magnesium powder (peach ring and chocolate sea salt), collagen powder (red velvet and salted caramel), Level-1 Protein Powder (milk chocolate or salted peanut butter)
- **Store-ground nut butters.** Our local store grinds their own nut butters with just salt, no added sugar or oils.
- **Dave's Killer Bread.** English muffins and sliced bread.
- **Meat, eggs, and poultry.** Locally raised and grass-fed for the best nutrients. (I can't always afford it, either. I buy it when I can, and then try to stock up.)
- **Milk frother.** FoodVille Rechargeable. It's charged via USB, the battery lasts a long time using it once daily, and there are two different attachments: a frother and a mini whisk.
- **Tea: Stash, Twinings, or Bigelow.** I'm no connoisseur, and I'm sure someone out there will have "better" recommendations. These are the brands I gravitate toward. I enjoy them, and they tend to fit my budget.
- **Coffee.** Locally roasted favorites: Fat Puppy and East Indies Coffee & Tea. Commercial brand: Maxwell House. Again, don't come for me. I do not claim to be a connoisseur or snob. Right now, these fit the budget, suit my taste, and do the job.

I had to stop looking at food as something bad. It does so much for the body; it's enjoyable, it's a means of celebration, and it's something pretty magical from growing, cultivating, purchasing, cooking, and consuming. I also had to look in the mirror and realize that I could be my own worst enemy or best friend, but the choice was mine. Was I going to continue to self-sabotage, or was I going to listen to my heart and choose differently?

Ever since I started working on my mental health with a therapist, I have slowly begun to change the way I deal with my nutrition. I started meal prepping several years ago, and that hasn't stopped. It makes my life easy to take one day a week, prepare all of my meals, and know that I'm set for the week ahead. I put less pressure on myself to be perfect, although the intrusive thoughts remain. I also am making slow changes to the foods I keep on hand.

I try to look at what I have to gain from the foods I'm buying to use in my recipes. I want to focus on health management, not solely weight management. Cutting whole food groups to focus on weight loss means losing opportunities to gain nutrients necessary for optimal health. Do I still use supplements and a few convenient items to help me fill nutritional gaps in the kitchen? Of course I do. Overall, I want my food to be my medicine and medicine to be my food.

To know more about my story or for additional tips, guidance, and recipes, follow me on Instagram: @kaitlynelysecoaching

Made in the USA
Columbia, SC
19 March 2025